Disruptive

7 Keys for Working Women Experiencing Hostile Environments

Goldyn P. Smith

Goldyn Standard Publishing Inc.

A subsidiary of The Goldyn Standard

Established and thriving in Atlanta, GA

Copyright © 2018 by Goldyn Standard Publishing. All rights reserved. No part of this publication may be reproduced, distributed, or transmitted in any form or by any means, including photocopying, recording, or other electronic or mechanical methods, without the prior written permission of the publisher, except in the case of brief quotations embodied in critical reviews and certain other noncommercial uses permitted by copyright law.

Disruptive: 7 Keys For Working Women Experiencing Hostile Environments

Author's photos taken by CJ Kanon

At Cam Kirk Studios

Atlanta, GA

ISBN - 9781717700919

Printed in the United States of America

Contents

Acknowledgments 4

Introduction 6

First things first - Navigating The Ever
Changing Work Environment 8

CHAPTER 01
I've Witnessed or Personally Experienced an Issue,
Do I Speak Out or Stay Silent About It? 10

CHAPTER 02
Document Everything To Protect Yourself............................... 22

CHAPTER 03
HR is In Place To Protect The Company, Not The Employee ... 28

CHAPTER 04
When To Decide To Seek Help Outside of The Company. 32

CHAPTER 05
Things to Consider When Choosing Legal Representation...... 41

CHAPTER 06
What To Expect If And When Litigation Begins..................... 49

CHAPTER 07
Keys to Keep in Mind while litigating 58

Bonus
My Appellate Experience 63

Epilogue.. 70

Acknowledgments

This book is dedicated to Miss Alberta. Mama, you're a mom to everyone who you encounter. I have strength, courage, wisdom and compassion because you set the example. Some of my earliest favorite memories is watching you work 3 jobs and running your business. Everything great about me is because of you.

To God - Be the glory. I thank you for all the strong women in my life. I thank you for being ever present in my life guiding me through the darkest moments which lead to this book.

To all the strong women who inspire me - Eve Poythress, Deborah Waller, Phyllis Daniels, Rita Andrews, Trina Allen, Valerie Hawkins, Roberta Shields, my aunties, grandmothers - Thank you.

To all the activists and allies, thank you for speaking truth to power and inspiring us to come forward and share our stories. I've been mostly inspired by Viola Davis, Sunny Hostin, Whoopi Goldberg, Maxine Waters, Angela Rye, Jamilah Lemieux, Oprah Winfrey, Valerie Jarrett, Brittany Packnett and Tamika Mallory. To everyone behind the Times Up and Me Too movements thank you.

To my tribe, the love, support and encouragement you give me is unmatched. The last 5 years have been the hardest of my life, this book serves as a testament to the strength of my support system. You all have seen me at my worst, cried with me while holding my hands at all hours of the day. There are not enough words to thank you all. Deb, Eve, CJ, Donnovan, David Bush, Cameron, Santos, Melody, Michael Andrew, Kelsey, Trevis, my family and anyone I forgot to name - thank you.

Special thanks to my mentors Robert Greene, Enitan Bereola and Karrine Steffans (Coach K).

This is for the countless women famous and non famous who have ever experienced issues at work and continued to stand strong. I hope this book helps to keep the conversation going.

Lastly, I dedicate this to my daddy who unquestionably believed in me, supported me and was the best father he could be to me. Rest well daddy, I got it from here.

Introduction

I didn't intend to write this book, I hesitated to share this part of my life so publicly. I battled with myself with constant internal conversations on whether I wanted to talk about this and if I did, how I wanted to. I started to write in my journal about this experience and what led me here as a way to give myself comfort. The last four years of my life were full up a lot of highs and devastating lows and instead of going to counseling I wrote my way through.

I was reluctant to share my experience because I'm a private person who has the public persona as a magazine publisher who makes things happen. Wanting to have certain parts of my life remain private, I decided against sharing. I had been approached by a few of my press club friends who asked me to share. I decided against letting anyone else controlling the way my experience is shared , so here we are.

Most books change the names to protect the innocent, this ain't that kind of book (thanks Jenifer Lewis). To give you the answer the question you're all wanting asking - the answer is no. I met Kalka years before I worked for him. I've shared meals with he & his wife, attended his father's funeral, shared in his excitement of becoming a new parent etc. I met Baer when he and Kalka became Kalka & Baer. Baer represented me in a personal injury lawsuit. I say all of that to state no - I didn't expect when I began to work for them things would go so terribly wrong. No, I definitely didn't believe in a million years I would experience the hostile work environment they cultivated within their firm. No, I didn't expect to be fired for calling out their willful wrongdoing, get fired and sue them in Federal District Court for racial discrimination, unpaid overtime and retaliation. Lastly, I certainly never thought I would have to appeal the Federal District Court's ruling especially after providing audio recordings and close to 500 pages of evidence including documents from the GA Department of Labor and more. I even submitted their testimony in their own words as part of my evidence which was "overlooked" by the District Court.

Here we are four years later with the case in the Court of Appeals due to the District Court ruling in their favor and not awarding me anything. I'll explain how that happened below.

I decided to share my experience in my own words not leaving it up to story editors at news stations etc. I shared my story via StoryCorps and my own podcast. I realized I could give women an insight to what life looks like once you speak up. I also wanted to share what I learned from litigating my case alone. There were a lot of lessons learned and I want to help people avoid some of the mistakes I made. I'm not an attorney, my only hope is to empower and equip you with the knowledge you may need to push through.

The justice system is flawed in many ways as it relates to ensuring equal protection under the law. I continuously try to balance emotion versus logic throughout my judicial process. It's not been easy, I've been angry, cried, even screamed throughout this process. I want you to know you're not alone and to understand it's a process. I've learned so much during this process that I'm sure many people wouldn't think was important. My case is now under the review of 3 judges at the 11th Circuit Court of Appeals. What happens next is up to God, here's my experience and what I learned.

First things first - navigating the ever changing work environment.

*I*n today's society, a lot of progress has taken place in workplaces nationwide. While there's been evolution in many ways, some things remain the same. Being a woman of color, there's a wide variety of microaggressions, inappropriate joking etc. I've experienced. Companies have slightly better policies than in the past however enforcement of policies are not always in effect. What's on paper is great, serious action is better when addressing employee grievances. We hear more stories of hostile work environments and the results of action or more often inaction by companies.

Work environment hostility, in my experience starts off with micro aggressions which grow into huge issues. All of which is preventable. Most of the aggressors know their actions or words are damaging. They take comfort in the mindset of it's no big deal and attempt to make their target look bad for speaking up. Aggressors feed off of power and the perception of having "the upper hand." Aggressors have the false perception of being untouchable.

It can be extremely difficult to navigate a hostile work environment. You consider all the ways things can go wrong and even worse lose you job. Some companies say they have "Open Door Policies" only to show you the door if you become too problematic. If you find yourself in a toxic, hostile work environment there are ways to navigate it. Here's my story and the things I learned along the way.

CHAPTER 01

I'VE WITNESSED OR PERSONALLY EXPERIENCED AN ISSUE, DO I SPEAK OUT OR STAY SILENT ABOUT IT?

We all have financial obligations to keep, you need your job to ensure things stay in place. There's not a person who doesn't understand that perspective. In some situations, there are instances you choose to overlook because you don't want to be "that person who can't take a joke" or "the person that's so sensitive". I've been there and even struggled with this same internal discussion. My situation was slightly different because I had personal relationships with these men for 7 years before working for them. In most cases, you don't know the people you go to work for. In my case I thought I did know them, which is why I never expected things to take the nasty turns it did when I began working for them. I overlooked a few things that made me take a beat and just filed it in my mental file cabinet as odd. I was there to work and understood the differences between business and personal.

In some cases, when you overlook comments, gestures, feelings and stay focused on the goal - things are manageable. In my experience, overlooking comments emboldened my employers and a few employees to become comfortable with their offenses. I will say this a few times throughout this book - aggressors never believe their behavior is inappropriate nor offensive. I would speak to my family and friends about the issues and try to get advice on how to deal with the micro aggressions. Those aggressions could range from inappropriate jokes and comments to physical touching and more.

As a woman of color in the workplace I feared looking like the angry black woman, especially being only one of two in the firm. My other co worker Eve, admitted she learned to grin and bear it most of the time and had admitted the political climate had made things worse. We often shared tips with each other on how to navigate the increasingly hostile environment. Being in a position where you experience or witness harassment, bullying, unwanted physical contact is difficult. It's not easy for anyone to go through especially feeling like speaking out will make things worse or you get fired. You have to weigh your options and decide the best course of action for you.

I made the decision to speak out once it was clear there was racial bias in my firm. I was extremely frustrated at the partners making myself and Eve, the only two black women in the office clean after everyone. It was demeaning especially knowing my grandmothers and great grandmothers spent years "cleaning up after white folks so you wouldn't have to." Kalka even sent an email stating "it's the price you pay for having new offices." His attitude was you do what I tell you and don't ever question it. He even said to me "this ain't Walmart" during a conversation we were having about the files in my office. It landed with me as he intended it to - condescending and offensive. I told him I never worked there and asked what he was implying to which he rolled his eyes and walked off. He frequently liked to make employees and clients feel beneath him. He bragged to myself and Eve about firing a former employee while opening mail "because she got pregnant and now she wants unemployment."

I was disgusted and frustrated about a lot of things. There were racial jokes and comments and I felt like the 9 year old me again. The current experiences in 2014 reminded of my first racist encounter as a child and how hurt and disappointed I was to experience it as an adult. I was a student at Perkerson Elementary School, and was given a safety patrol position. My teacher nominated me because he said he thought I was likable enough that students would listen to me. It was a warm spring day, the bell rang and everyone headed to class. There were always students who lingered, I always gave students time.

A few minutes had gone by, I noticed a group of 3 boys. I said hey guys get to class. The boys chuckled as I walked closer and said again, y'all have to clear the hallway. The white boy in the group turned to me and said I don't have to do what you say nigger, get out of my face! I was shocked at the face he got in my face pushed his chest against mine and repeated it again. "I don't have to do what you say nigger, get out of my face! The other two boys ran, tears welled up in my eyes and I grabbed him by his arm to take him to the principal. He pulled his arm away, I grabbed him by his shirt and proceeded to drag him down the hall.

He fell to the floor, I kept dragging as he hit lockers, door stops and all. I had tunnel vision as I headed to the principal's office. I opened the door the the office and I screamed he called me nigger and pushed me! The ladies ran to me to comfort me and that's when I noticed the boy was bleeding and I told the administrator. She grabbed tissue, gave it to him and continued talking to me. I told them what happened and told them I didn't want to get in trouble but he started it. They calmed me down and sent me back to class. Next thing I know his parents were there and I told my mom what happened. It's hard to put into words the way I felt about it then and now. It's even more painful thinking about my mom's disappointed face. Her disappointment wasn't in me, it was in the situation and us being so young having that experience.

I share that experience to illustrate how as a little black girl being raised in the South, you have an experience like that - it hurts and its shocking. As I grew up, I experienced many more and became thick skinned but more aware of the possibilities of encountering racism whether it was small or large. Some micro agressions constantly remind you racism still exists, you overlook micro aggressive actions because you're just trying to make it through the day.

There's a lot of connotations and coded language people with prejudices and bigotry use especially in this day and age. I would often hear offensive prejudice jokes within the office by one or both partners about clients, other attorneys etc. I took mental notes and kept moving because it wasn't directed at me.

My breaking point was when I was asked to clean a trial exhibit and make it shiny. There were other ladies in the office who were already in the office that could do it. Our boss specifically called my coworker to have her direct me to do it. When I asked Eve why the other girls weren't asked, she said you know they think we're the help. I made so much noise and complained so loudly while cleaning it that Baer came out of his office and the other girls did too. I finished and told them I was going to get something out of my car and left out of the office. Upset and completely disgusted, I spoke to Renee Smith (Morgan) a female attorney at the firm who was third in charge. During our conversation she admitted she thought it was wrong but if I wasn't happy I could find other employment. At that point, I decided to stay while looking for other employment. Kalka was unhappy with my "lackluster cleaning" he asked Eve to do it and she did. She was visibly upset we went to lunch, no one asked us to do anything else that day. We both decided to stop cleaning the office and let chips fall where they may.

Neither of us used the break room so we were unaware dishes were piled up, coffee was spilled onto the counters until a firm email went out about it. No one replied to the email, so another one came announcing one of the other girls would take over keeping the break room tidy and keeping it stocked. Small victory but it was the calm before the storm.

It was always a tense environment whenever racial "jokes and observations" were made. There were other instances like inviting everyone to lunch at the country club except for Eve and I and sending us home for the day. Other instances include calling a black woman Precious telling her to calm down to demean her or calling clients "broke black crackhead bitches" in various email exchanges. There were questions like "Why is it the first thing black people do is buy a car instead of buying property with their settlement?" As we would leave for the day we would be told to "stay black." Oh and there was the chicken wing email, let me explain. After Eve & I stopped cleaning, the fridge wasn't cleaned out and there was a smell. The partners sent a nasty email to us and the firm that shared our suite to say whoever had the chicken wings needed to remove them. One of the African American attorneys from the other firm came to Eve and I and said y'all need to go get your wings laughing at the angry tone of the email. Eve and I knew it wasn't ours even though we were suspected. Finally, Renee confessed after a few hours later that they were hers and apologized to everyone.

I would never advise you to immediately quit your job, although I do understand the urge to curse everyone out and storming out. There's a lot that comes with reporting hostility, it's not an easy decision. What made this situation complicated for me was I saw none of this until I worked there. Weigh your options and decide how you want to move forward. Make a plan, adjust it accordingly and always remember your peace of mind is worth more than anything else.

While continuing my employment search, things became increasingly uncomfortable and even more inappropriate. The firm had christened Friday's as Beer & Wine Fridays which was the suggestion of Renee, who had her purchase list ready. I was asked numerous times to stop at a bottle shop to bring in Miller Genuine Draft for the partners. I was always uncomfortable making beer purchases at 8:30 am, I was told it was "part of my weekly duties." Everyone indulged except myself and my Eve, it didn't sit well with us. The working environment slowly turned into fraternity house culture with the abuse of drugs, alcohol and prescription drugs by others in our firm. I was offered "treats" but always declined. I like to keep my work environment sober.

There were two specific events that happened that really changed everything. The firm had been working hard on a personal injury trial, to make sure we were victorious and our client was happy. The trial involved the motorcycle I had to "clean and make it shiny." One December afternoon, all staff members received a victory email and an invitation to a local restaurant to celebrate. Eve was extremely reluctant to go, I convinced her to go have 1 drink. As we all packed up to leave I chose to ride with Eve. We arrived at the restaurant where we were greeted by bar staff who invited us in. We spotted Renee at the bar and Baer came to greet us. As he was talking about the favorable judgement, he accidentally brushed Eve's butt. He immediately apologized, Eve told him she didn't notice. He then grabbed a handful and laughed asking you feel that? He then walked away laughing. I immediately became enraged and made eye contact with Renee her eyes wide and upset. I looked at Eve and said let's go. Before we could leave, Kalka came over and smacked Eve on her butt and told us to grab another drink.

At that point, all I could think was to get her out of there immediately. Her hands were shaking, she was so upset as we waited for valet I tried to keep her calm. We were both upset, angry, confused etc. We made it back to my car and sat for a while trying to process what just happened. I wasn't sure where to go from there. Throughout the weekend I kept replaying it in my mind and wondering what I could've done to protect Eve more.

I returned to work and everyone asked where Eve was. As if they didn't know or understand why she needed time off. We attended the company Christmas party at one of the partner's homes as a mandatory requirement to get our bonus. A few people chose to play Cards Against Humanity, Eve and I went to the basement where we played Wii bowling with others until it was time for bonuses. The partners came to find us and went went upstairs for their speech and our checks.

When I returned to work, I asked to speak to Renee in her office. Knowing from previous experience how she could twist conversations, I took my phone which was recording our conversation. I told her Eve was reluctant to return to work due to the assault at the happy hour event. Renee became immediately defensive and stated "If she tries to sue, she will have to prove there was a pattern of harassment." When she made the statement, I recalled how Renee would frequently tell us how important it was for her to get her name on the door. She was set "on doing whatever it takes to have my name added to K&B as a partner." A little shocked by her defensive stance, I told her no one said anything about suing anyone.

I asked her what the grievance policy or procedure is when a conflict happens. She did not have an answer, and proceeded to minimize the actions of the men. The intensity of our conversation began to escalate when I told her how wrong it was. She asked if she could convince them to apologize to Eve if I thought it would make a difference. I told her it would be a start but I couldn't speak for Eve. I had known and been best friends with Eve for over a decade, I was and still protective of her. I told Renee we all have jobs we need and bills we have to pay and I hoped for a resolution. An important note here, the firm did not have a Human Resources department. In the next few chapters, I'll explain the reason what that matters. Eve returned to work and met with Renee and the others on her own. I don't know what the conversations were and still don't.

A few weeks later, a celebration invite was sent out and Renee asked if we were going. I didn't reply to the email, and in Renee's response to Eve she said "protect the butt" as a joke. Neither of us saw anything funny but it was interesting she did. From that point forward, I limited my interactions with Renee. You can't talk about girl power one moment and make a joke about an assault the next moment. There is nothing funny or lighthearted about sexual assault, harassment, bullying women in the workplace and it never will be. On the

Friday before the King holiday, I was in Eve's office asking if we had to work. Here in Atlanta, the day is significant with lots of celebrations and community service. Renee walked in, sat down to join the conversation. As we began to talk about how the firm handles the holiday Renee stated "Eve, I was told by Kalka you get the day off because you're black." I chimed in and asked if it was true, Renee repeated the statement and gestured to me "you get it off too since you're black." I walked out went back to my office. As I mentioned it to a few other coworkers they were upset. They were upset because they had to work and found it unfair the black women had the day off. After Laura and Haley confronted Baer about it, Kalka sent an email that Sunday evening telling everyone to enjoy the day off. As you can see over a period of weeks, the environment became increasingly hostile.

We went from 1099 employees to W2 employees that January. Baer's father who was an attorney and judge visited us and told us to be sure we were being paid for overtime. Baer's mom came a couple weeks later to tour the office and she asked me "why do they have you set up in a closet?" I told her I wasn't sure, smiled and made polite conversation. As she was saying her goodbyes, she told us about her state court duties. She was and is a practicing attorney as well, she offered a ladies lunch one day soon. We all jumped on the invite and before she left she told us make sure you're getting paid for overtime girls, she left as we looked at each other. In our team meeting, I asked about not being paid overtime, Baer told us we weren't eligible for overtime due to the administrative exemption. I didn't question it at the time, I should have.

A couple weeks later while gathering paycheck stubs to show proof of income I discovered what I believed was an error. My hourly rate was incorrect. I reached out to payroll to verify they were aware of the issue. Their response in a email was "your hourly rate was "The reason you received a discounted hourly rate for that period was because of the addition of employer payroll taxes associated with your employment status. In 2013, when you were a contractor, you were paying 100% of payroll/self employment taxes. As an employer, Kalka Baer began paying ½ of your payroll taxes in 2014. To keep your net compensation level, your pay rate was discounted slightly in consideration of payroll taxes. For any additional information, you should talk with Baer."

I sent an email with everyone attached and confirmed to them I wasn't made aware I would have to pay employment taxes. There were two reasons I sent a company wide email neither one was malicious.

- I wasn't sure if any other employees had the issue and wanted to make them aware.

- I wanted everyone to understand I wasn't aware of the tax issue and wanted them to see the payroll company's response.

I received 7 back to back calls from the office while out on lunch after I sent the email. There were a couple of responses to my email. I called Baer back and got an earful while he screamed at me they don't steal from employees. He went on a rant for about 10 minutes and hung up. Eve and I finished outlet lunches and headed back. We finished the day without any more confrontations. The next day, I received an email from Baer about a case update meeting, I prepared to go the meeting. I walked in and we spoke about various cases and I gave status updates. As we were wrapping up I could tell he was increasingly agitated. He stood up and began yelling at me in his office, saying I accused him of stealing from the employees. I told him I thought we resolved this. He continued to scream and rant like a maniac to the point where employees came out of their offices. He walked closer and stood over me and leaned into my face saying he wanted to tell me to my face how unprofessionally I handled the issue. He continued to yell until I stood up to walk out as I stood toe to toe with him, I told him I never accused them of stealing from us. I gave him the option to send me back to my office or home. I walked out and went back to my office and then down to my car.

The hostile environment had hit a nuclear level and I wasn't sure what would happen next. I finished my open cases for the day and went home. I called the IRS because I wanted to understand my liability and wanted to ensure the change wouldn't affect my rates. They emailed a brochure, Eve asked for a copy I emailed to her. The rest of that week was full of confrontation leading up to a mandatory firm meeting in which we were all fired.

Takeaway- There are a few takeaways from this experience that surprised even me.

A. For every action, there is a reaction - We learned this in school for every cause, there is an effect. A lot transpired that I didn't raise a concern about before speaking out. In the workplace, you have to learn to juggle all the personalities and idiosyncrasies. You're not going to like every single thing, person or company procedure. With any job, you learn to navigate the environment. I spoke out when I felt I was being singled out and treated unfairly. Eve and I were the only employees given the responsibility of keeping the office clean. Kalka said it was the price we had to pay for our new offices. Yes he actually said that in an email to Eve and verbally to me when speaking about the kitchenette. When Eve and I decided to stop cleaning, that's when the issues started to escalate. When Eve came to me to tell me Kalka requested I clean the motorcycle- that was the straw. The other women in the office weren't asked, only Eve and I. When I spoke up, I was met with resistance from Renee who told me I could always work somewhere else.

B. The company didn't have a grievance procedure - Out of all the companies I've worked for before and after K&B, they were the only company that had no handbook nor policies. Even more surprising because they are attorneys. The response I received when I asked about this was they are a boutique firm that's "like a small family." In every other job I've had, new employees receive handbooks during orientation. As they say hindsight is 20/20 and this issue should have been a red flag.

At the time I was fired, I knew I documented everything, not understanding how important that would be in my case against K&B. I didn't know how much of my experience depended on documentation with the EEOC, the state Department of Labor, the United States Department of Labor, State of GA Department of Revenue etc. I expected K&B to lie about the whole ordeal because they had and have an image to protect. Some would think being fired was the end, for me it was the beginning of a very long process to making sure I cleared my name on as many records as needed and hold K&B accountable.

CHAPTER 02

DOCUMENT EVERYTHING TO PROTECT YOURSELF

You've made your plan, you've made some decisions on what to do. The most important thing you can do is document everything and not on your work devices. Keep a journal, hold on to emails, anything that you can have as proof of the hostility you're experiencing.

In my case, I always use my app on my phone to record my classes, interviews I do with my magazine etc. Recording was the way I chose to document everything. I didn't research the law before I started recording because I needed proof. Some states have strict rules on recording conversations, my state was not one of them. Additionally, I never considered I would need to use them. I recorded meetings and conversations with the Renee after she twisted my words when I complained about cleaning. If I didn't record, I always had someone as a witness who I trusted would tell the truth.

In most cases that I've experienced, when you complain about an issue it will be your word against theirs. Unless you have the proof to support your claims, a record will be made and things go back to semi normal.

In other cases, and in my own experience things get progressively worse. For example, after my initial complaint my employers and employees began to joke about my concerns. Always keep in mind how important it is to keep a record of your experiences. In my case, I never had a Human Resources department to report the issues to. My bosses always took pride and comfort in that which lead them to brag about how they couldn't be sued. Needless to say, they were wrong. I continued to document until I was fired.

This book serves as a testimony to how important documentation is because without it I wouldn't be where I am and you wouldn't be reading this. The question I was asked the most throughout this pursuit was - "Why did you record conversations and meetings?" I decided to start recording, not to catch anybody doing anything but just to have a record of meetings because I hate taking notes.

Once I filed for unemployment, a lot of accusations were made for example - I abandoned my job by not showing up to work, I was a problematic employee and I violated company policies. None of which were true, I gave them the opportunity to change their statements to the DOL. They insisted to the DOL in writing and under the penalty of perjury their statements were true. They signed the documents stating I wasn't entitled to payments. There was also some unexpected things that took place, before I sent in my proof. The DOL had a hard time verifying I even worked at K&B. Unaware of what was happening, I was contacted by a caseworker who asked if I could send my paycheck stubs. I sent them in an asked why they needed them, I was then told when I filed for benefits, there was no record.

An investigation had been launched once I filed for unemployment. I apologized to my caseworker because I didn't know my filing would cause an investigation, I only wanted to get my payments due to being fired. The investigation took 9 weeks after my initial filing and during that time, the DOL advised me to seek legal counsel and file a complaint with the EEOC. At that point, I knew whatever they were investigating was a big deal. The last thing my case worker told me on that call was to also contact the IRS. I told her I already had due to the payroll error and sent the brochure they sent me to the other employees. She repeated to me again to retain a lawyer as fast as I could and contact the EEOC.

After getting over the initial shock of what my case worker told me, I took her advice and immediately sought counsel and filed with the EEOC. K&B continued to send in documents to the DOL which would send a copy to me to verify if they were legitimate. Some were and some weren't. I told the DOL I had documents and recordings to disprove their account. I was awarded my benefits and continued to move forward with speaking with the EEOC on my racial discrimination and retaliation claim. I told them I was seeking legal representation for the unpaid overtime I never received payment for and completed their filing procedures.

A couple weeks later, I received a letter from the DOL stating K&B was challenging my payments. They repeated themselves in documents I abandoned my position when I didn't return to work. I told my case worker to standby and while we were on the call, I emailed her my proof. What K&B didn't expect or see coming was I had quite a few emails and the recording of the meeting where we were all fired. The emails proved I was in fact a great employee with praise and offer of a raise for the great job I was doing. The recording was K&B shouting and screaming at all of the women employees about the "drama" that was being caused, the amount of money they had to pay (to correct their payroll error) and disputes between Renee and Haley. None of which had anything to do with me or Eve, in the recording you could also hear both K&B fire all of us. My case worker reviewed my proof and told me I was required to send them what I sent to her and reconfirmed my date and time for our hearing.

The DOL called to start the hearing and as I waited for the adjudicator to confirm everyone's presence and administer the oath, a calm feeling flushed over me. I knew the proof I submitted was all I needed to prove they were in fact lying about how my employment ended. As I began to testify and share my account, K&B disconnected the call. Unsure of what happened, the adjudicator stopped me and told me their line disconnected and she would need to place me on hold to call them. I was sure it was intentional even though I knew the adjudicator was unsure. She called back and we resumed the hearing. Once my testimony was over, they started off saying "we no longer wish to challenge her benefits" which caught us all off guard. The adjudicator asked him to repeat himself so she could be sure she heard him. Baer repeated "we no longer wish to stop her from getting her benefits, I would like an opportunity to dispute everything she said."

The adjudicator then explained to him if he didn't want to continue the hearing she could adjourn but this wasn't the time or place to dispute. She offered him a chance to testify and give his account of what happened. After a few moments, Baer agreed to testify. He answered a series of questions and the adjudicator asked "Was she fired?" Baer confirmed I was fired but he didn't fire me Kalka did. The adjudicator asked the reason I was fired and Baer refused to give a reason due to self incrimination. Baer then proceeded to speak about things off topic when the adjudicator had to remind him this hearing was about unemployment benefits only. Baer gave his last words of testimony, I gave mine and the adjudicator stated she would mail a decision.

A few weeks later, I received a letter confirming I was entitled to the payments received and the remainder of the payments I had not received. A few days later, I received a letter from the DOL I didn't expect. The letter confirmed that I was misclassified as an independent contractor during my employment with K&B. The letter confirmed that not only would they correct that for me but

Disruptive

also any employee past, present or future. Later that week I received my Right to Sue letter from the EEOC confirming I could pursue legal action against K&B for my claims of racial discrimination, retaliation and violating the Fair Labor and Standards Act.

Takeaways:

A. Without proof it's your word vs. theirs - It's important to keep this in mind because even if you reported your complaint verbally to someone they can always deny it. I've been in positions and seen instances where someone you thought you trusted to have your back didn't. There is no minimum amount of proof or too much. All that matters is you have something. Remember, emails can serve a proof. Most of the time, it's preferable to have proof in writing.

B. Always retain a copy of your proof - You always retain the originals. When you Report an issue, you never know who may need to see your documents. In my case, there were a lot of government agencies asking for my proof as well as court officials. Some of the proof I had was being used in other litigation against the firm. I was asked to provide documents or consent to my documents being used in those other proceedings. There were also some instances where I was told to be prepared to testify, I never considered other proceedings. I was prepared because I retained my originals.

C. Even the things you don't think are important can become vital - Small details to you could make the difference. For instance, when I contacted the IRS about the tax structure I asked for brochures I could keep. I wanted to understand how and if K&B's actions would affect my tax filing. I was telling Eve about it and she asked me to email it to her. I sent the email and thought nothing else of it. What I later learned was when I sent that email I engaged in "protective activity."

Protective activity explained by the National Labor Relations Board is described as : talking with one or more coworkers about your wages and benefits or other working conditions, circulating a petition asking for better hours, participating in a concerted refusal to work in unsafe conditions, and joining with coworkers to talk directly to your employer, to a government agency etc. My attorney was so excited I sent that email, I was horrified I mistakenly sent it to Eve's work email instead of personal. My attorney explained that by sending that email and sharing that information with Eve my employer violated the FLSA by firing me. He further explained that would be our grounds to sue for wrongful termination and retaliation. Documentation is key, small things can become major.

CHAPTER 03

HR IS IN PLACE TO PROTECT THE COMPANY, NOT THE EMPLOYEE

*H*uman Resources is in place to protect the company's interest. How many times have you heard someone say they went to HR for an issue and it wasn't resolved? Companies employ HR professionals to help enforce policies with employees. That's why you receive the employee handbook. In rare cases, you may see policies change and handbooks updated. When changes happen with a company's policies, there's a serious reason. Changes affect policies - it can be state or federal labor laws, managerial or due to litigation. As an employee, you don't consider why the policy changed you're just told when it becomes effective. As I've been on my litigation path, I've become more aware of how many companies are being sued for not following their own policies.

In my current litigation against K&B, I learned through the course of our litigation how vital it is to have a HR department. What our judges couldn't believe was there was no employee handbook. The state's labor department thought I was joking when I testified before their adjudicator there was no handbook. That's not a joke, yes I worked for attorneys who did not have an HR department nor employee handbook. They who used the brag to all of us that we couldn't sue them because there was no

HR. They learned how wrong they were publicly during the course of litigation. In their sworn testimony, they stated I abandoned my job. When that argument didn't work, they stated I violated company policies. When they were asked to name the policy, they were unable to. It's hard to make most of your defense about violating company policies when there is no handbook. Beyond that, most sensible companies have handbooks and policies.

Most common policies like Open Door can sometimes have an unexpected affect on your standing with the company. On the other hand, there are Human Resources managers/ employees who are interested in helping employees - it's rare. If you have great HR professionals who have great conflict resolution skills consider yourself lucky. Either way, there's some tips I can share with you to protect yourself and your rights as an employee.

Takeaways -

A. Your initial complaint to HR should always be in writing. Verbal complaints to HR are fine, written are better. I've learned this lesson the hard way watching friends go through various incidents in the workplace. When airing your grievances with a coworker or HR professional, verbal communications can quickly turn into your word versus theirs. Writing your complaint and sending by email helps you because you have written proof of your complaint with a time and date stamp. It's hard to dispute the written word. Having friends and sometimes strangers as me for advice, this is the key I share with them. Once you have sent your email, the ball is placed and n HR's court to review and contact you to follow up. You will most likely receive a prompt response to your complaint because it is in writing. The HR response may be in writing on you may be asked to come in to speak. The critical thing to keep in my is to document your meeting with HR. In the state I live in the law is a one party law which states you can record and not notify the other party or parties. Other states require both parties to be made aware. Depending on your perspective that can be a good or bad thing. If recording with your phone or other device is not feasible. Take a witness you trust or take lots of notes. Questions you should always ask HR are:

- What can I expect from this grievance process?
- What does the review process include?
- Who will you speak with besides me?
- Will there be a record of this grievance in my HR file?
- How long will this process take?
- What are the next steps?
- If I'm not happy with the resolution what are my options?

B. Plan for the best, prepare for the worst - Set realistic expectations of what you hope to gain from notifying HR. Once your meeting has concluded, take a break to make notes of things you were ok with during the meeting and what concerns you were left with. I can't emphasize enough how important it is to remain professional throughout this step. It's extremely easy to become frustrated, discouraged, angry, hurt and disappointed. It's natural to feel that way and your feelings about your ordeal are valid. Remember that while going through this process. If things are resolved to the point where you can bear it that's fantastic. You also have to prepare for things to not go as you expected.

C. Remain professional even if you don't like HR's response - This process will require you to be professional in moments when you will want to curse everyone out. Waiting for or getting HR's response may be one of those moments. In other jobs I've had when HR was involved, things sometimes went unexpectedly and things were said in the heat of the moment. One person's opinion and honesty can be insubordination in the eyes of an employer. Listen to respond, not to argue and take time to process the information you are given and plan your next step. If things are resolved to your satisfaction that's great.

CHAPTER 04

WHEN TO DECIDE TO SEEK HELP
OUTSIDE OF THE COMPANY.

There are a myriad of reasons to consider seeking help outside of your company. The first time and only time I sought assistance outside of K&B was when I contacted the IRS. Still employed at that time, I was concerned about my tax liability due to K&B's payroll error. K&B's payroll person told me the hourly rate was reduced to cover payroll taxes. Not disputing whether or not it was true Once I emailed the documents I received from the IRS, Eve asked for a copy and I sent it. Earlier, I explained how vital that small detail was.

Both times I was berated by Baer, I recorded it. As the in office ambush took place other employees cane out of their offices to see what was going on. The only person who didn't come out was Kalka, most likely because he encouraged Baer. Baer told me he wanted "put me in my place and tell me to my face" how he didn't appreciate me calling them thieves. I stood up to get my things and told him to either send me to my office or send me home because this conversation was over. He stood there shocked, I walked out slamming his door and walked past my office to the elevator.

Goldyn P. Smith

Wednesday morning I received an email from Kalka telling me to be prepared for a meeting that afternoon. As the time approached, I sent an email asking if he was ready. I received an email from him an hour later saying he would need to reschedule. Less than 48 hours after receiving hat email I was fired but I wasn't the only one. It wasn't until after speaking with a couple of attorney friends, I began to understand why K&B was so upset about it.

When I went in to work that morning, the environment was more icy than usual. That afternoon, Baer sent an email with an apology but more. In the email, Baer K&B was accused of stealing from their employees which was something they would never do. The email continued to explain it was an error and they were working hard on a resolution. We all knew it was a tactic to do damage control. The one line that stood out to me the most was - the issue was brought to his attention by another employee before I asked about it. I had to read that line twice because they way K&B both exploded on me and antagonized me that whole week about it floored me. It lead me to ask if these questions:

- Since the "payroll error" had been brought to them before, why wasn't it corrected?

- Why was I verbally attacked, bullied, intimidated and humiliated in front of the whole office?

Thursday of that crazy week was pretty uneventful, no one spoke to me and I was fine with that. I responded to emails as needed and spoke to lots of clients that day. The only strange thing was, the lady I shared an office with resigned. She came in, told me what she was about to do and hugged me. She showed me her client files and where to find everything and she went to talk to Baer. I was a little surprised about her resignation. She was a law student who worked less than 20 hours per week and had missed some time. She came from a wealthy family and didn't need to

Disruptive

work but I sensed something else had happened. I had been copied on a email where the partners were nasty toward her about being out. I asked why she was resigning, she told me it had a lot to do with Baer.

She referenced a few times they were at the country club and Baer referenced marriage and intimacy issues. I'll leave it there due to it being a sensitive subject and out of respect for Baer's family. The student also spoke about the inappropriate conversations and jokes that made her uncomfortable. I told her I understood and we both agreed about the lack of professionalism in the office and the frat house culture. We all received an email from Baer that it would be her last day and Baer being himself made a joke that wasn't appropriate. She said her goodbyes and left. I was sad but we had each other's numbers so it was fine.

Mandatory firm meeting - Friday morning started off like any other, beer and wine were brought in and the day started. Once Eve and I got settled in, she noticed someone had been on her computer. She called me to her office where she showed me an email from October had been forwarded to Kalka a few hours before we got in. Eve was extremely upset because she knew she didn't send it to Kalka.

A few weeks earlier, the partners demanded everyone's computer passwords. Their position was the computers belonged to them and we should provide the information. I didn't argue it, I didn't provide my password either. One day after leaving the office, Renee called stating she needed to use my computer to print something and asked for my password. I declined to give it to her, she pressed for about 10 minutes and became angry. I gave it to her, the following day I came in and changed it. A couple days later, Renee called saying I tried to use the scanner again but the password didn't work. She asked if I changed it, I told her I did and when she asked for it I refused and told her I would see her tomorrow. No one else demanded my password again.

I reminded Eve of that while we tried to figure out why of all the emails that particular one was forwarded to Kalka. We knew it was an act of messiness because the email was poking fun at another employee's LSAT scores. Renee admitted in the email her and the other employee has been hanging out drinking in the office. Renee emailed Eve and was laughing about "the bitch's LSAT score was super low." Eve responded and told them to enjoy the night. That was in October, now in February this email is an issue.

Around 10am, we all received an email stating there would be a mandatory firm meeting at 12:15. Less than two minutes later, Renee frantically knocked on my door asking to come in. Before I could ask what was wrong, she blurted out "I'm so sorry, I betrayed your confidence and told K&B you came to me about their grabbing of Eve." She became hysterical as she profusely apologized and kept saying she thinks we're all getting fired. I told her we should go to Eve's office so she could tell her what happened in her conversation with K&B. She told Eve about the conversation she had with them earlier that week. You read that correctly, Renee had just told us on Friday 2 hours before the mandatory meeting about her conversation with K&B about me reporting the sexual assault to her. She apologized, continued to cry and left me and Eve to discuss everything. Eve and I took a walk to talk about things. I reminded Eve that I recorded the conversation because I knew Renee was known to not be truthful about her part in situations in the past. Eve and I went back to work and waited for the meeting.

All of us ladies gathered in the conference room and made small talk about Renee's wedding planning and about good shows to watch. While we waited, I got a call and returned to the conference room. As we sat and waited, Renee played around with the Apple TV remote and we watched music videos. K&B came in and started the meeting.

K& B started the meeting off talking about the unnecessary drama that happened all week and their frustration at the money they've had to pay and what it costed them. The began to scream how the firm was a place for business and while there is not for wedding planning nor gossiping. Kalka stated they don't care about child care issues, caretaker doctor appointments or LSAT scores. I'm a full time caretaker for my mom, Eve is a mom, Renee was planning a wedding and Haley was retaking the LSAT. K&B was personally attacking each of us as they continued to talk about how there had been too much drama. Kalka told us of all the resumes he gets daily and how we were all replaceable. Kalka continued "As far as I'm concerned, you're all canned. Go back to your offices, pack your things and go. Your computers, phones and emails are locked, go home." We all got up to go back to our offices, Renee kept apologizing. An attorney who shared outlet suite asked what happened and I told him we were all just fired. He asked if I was serious, I confirmed and he gave me a business card and told me to email my resume to him and he could try to help. I thanked him, waited for Eve and we left. Eve had been with the firm the longest even before Kalka partnered with Baer and she was shocked. It was over, as she drove I started to email my resume and notified a few attorneys I was no longer with the firm and where their files were located in my office. Eve and I went to lunch and once I got home, I applied for unemployment online and continued reaching out to recruiters. A few of the attorneys I worked for through K&B offered their apologies and offered assistance with finding a new position. I continued to look for work while the unemployment process started.

Going outside of your employer can be as risky sometimes and cause more issues. As you saw above, things escalated quickly into a perfect storm of mess. Readjust your expectations so you won't be caught off guard. I definitely felt blindsided by the whole email drama and mandatory meeting. I never expected for all of us to be fired on the same day all at once for the reasons we were. I was extremely upset at Renee because she knew what she did but didn't tell me. Even now, I have no idea what Renee told them, I wasn't given a chance of rebuttal to anything she said in her meeting with them. In hindsight, I believe I was fired for not only whatever Renee said in her meeting but also my contact with the IRS.

I wanted to understand more about it and what the IRS may require from me. I never looked at it like I was reporting K&B. My perspective was I pay enough in taxes, I don't want to pay more than what's required. Who wants to pay more taxes than they should? K&B saw my contact with the IRS and sharing the information as an aggressive tactic although that wasn't my intent.

There are steps you can take to protect yourself if you do decide to seek help outside of your company whether you've gone to HR or not. In some instances, you may feel uneasy about going to HR. Below are a few resources.

- Contacting the EEOC - The EEOC handles **complaints of employment discrimination.** Filing a complaint with the EEOC is time sensitive. If you work for a private company your time to file is 180 days from the date of incident. If you work for a state or federal agency, you have **300 days** to file a charge. You can find information on their site on the process of filing the charge, what you will need and what you can expect. Your goal is to get the Right to Sue letter (which takes time) from them before starting any legal action. If you're employed and are fired, you must notify them so they can instruct you accordingly. Their website is https://www.eeoc.gov/.

Disruptive

- Contacting the NLRB - The National Labor Relations Board is an independent federal agency that investigates charges that allege unfair labor practices. You do not have to belong to a union for them to help you. This was a resource I was unaware of until I hired my second attorney. The NLRB fights on behalf of the employee and ensures the employee's rights are not violated. You can eFile or you can schedule an appointment with a local office to get assistance with your issue. Their website is https://www.nlrb.gov/.

- Contacting State or Federal DOL - Your local Department of Labor can help with unemployment benefits assistance, referrals for new jobs, and classes and training. If you have concerns about your wages like I did, your local DOL may refer you to the USDOL and you can find resources there and file complaints there to get assistance with your issue. If they can't help you, you can ask for suggestions which they can help you with.

Takeaways -

A. Expect the unexpected - Throughout this process, I always felt a range of emotions about how things went and then I would find out something else. As I mentioned earlier, I filed for unemployment online and followed the instructions I was given about the weekly requirements. I didn't expect to get a call from them stating they could not locate my wages in their system. I had worked, been paid, received check stubs and everything I told them they were wrong. I asked them to send me a copy of what they had, once I saw K&B wasn't listed as my employer at all I knew something was wrong. I took all of my documents to the local office and gave them stubs, 1099s, a few of my company business cards along with the driver's license. I waited a few hours to be seen because I was in such disbelief. When I was able to speak to someone, they explained they only knew about Kalka's solo practice and not K&B and had no record of it. I began to get upset and asked what that meant for my benefits and explained to them about the "payroll error." They asked if I had documents to prove it, I gave it to them and they referred me to the USDOL. That's when I knew this was going to get bad for K&B and become a lengthy process. I didn't expect any of this and really didn't want to expose anything else I just wanted my benefits. GDOL understood my reluctance, they made copies of my documents and told me to keep up my weekly reports while they made a decision on benefits. As the weeks went by, they asked for more documents - I knew K&B were in serious trouble. The GDOL sent me copies of the documents they received from K&B and asked me if they were correct. Some were, some were not and I provided my proof to counter what they sent. It took 10 weeks to receive my first benefit payment, K&B contested it and we were set for a hearing. Baer confirmed I was fired but stated Kalka fired all of us. When asked the reason, Baer refused to give one due to self incrimination. I continued to get my benefits and hired an attorney.

B. You will learn a lot about Employee's Rights - When you start looking for help outside of your company, you will learn the good, bad and ugly about your rights. Some states gives the employees more rights than others. At Will employment means you or your employer have the right to terminate your employment with or without reason at any time. Employees cannot be terminated because they have complained about any activities that violate state or federal law that they have observed in the workplace (e.g. discriminatory conduct or sexual harassment). In addition, you can also not be terminated for participating in activities that are an extension of your legal rights. Your local DOL can give you more information along with the state's employment laws.

C. Ask for referrals from resources - Agencies like the EEOC can provide you with a list of attorneys who can possibly assist you. The NLRB can give you referrals to agencies they work with that can assist you with your complaint. Most of them will tell you they can not give legal advice, they can point you in the right direction. The question I asked was if you were in my shoes what would you do? Their answers usually gave me the answers I needed, I encourage you to try that question to help you along.

CHAPTER 05

THINGS TO CONSIDER WHEN CHOOSING LEGAL REPRESENTATION

*A*fter, taking the advice of the GDOL to find an attorney, I began my research. Seems like it would be easy to find a great employment law attorney in Atlanta. I was quite surprised when I was met with so much rejection. After receiving a few rejections, I was surprised of the answer. "You're a paralegal seeking an attorney who will help you sue other attorneys (K&B). Lawyers don't like going after other lawyers which is why you keep getting the "we have a conflict" answer." Admittedly, I was shocked and really discouraged. I asked the EEOC for their suggested list of attorneys. I started to work the list, I was still met with we decline representation. I was so upset and frustrated, I took a break from the search. I started to look at attorneys outside of Atlanta, I was still met with rejection. I expanded the search to out of state and still wasn't successful. It seemed impossible to find an attorney to take my case. My inbox began to fill up with multiple declines. I was stuck, I began to consider representing myself. I frequently thought of that famous quote by Abraham Lincoln who was also an attorney "He who represents himself has a fool for a client."

I didn't know the first thing about employment law, I worked in personal injury and had light knowledge of workers compensation.

One thing I felt good about was my evidence and my ability to complete lengthy research and take really great notes. My outlook on this experience changed once I received my Right To Sue letter from the EEOC. It was truly a game changer because they looked at my proof and decided to grant me the right to sue K&B. It also helped that K&B didn't feel it was worth their time to provide the documents EEOC requested. Instead, I received text messages with photos of K&B making a mockery of my EEOC complaint by posting it to the break room fridge for all to see. K&B treated the EEOC the same flippant way as they did the GDOL.

I researched cases similar to my own, read countless briefs and began to organize my evidence. I requested official copies of all documents, recording of hearings and investigation results. Through my research, I started to find my experience was was more common than I initially believed. There are countless stories of hostile work environments, the issues that created the hostility and shocking accounts of bullying, harassment, retaliation and more. After sending a few more emails seeking representation, an attorney responded asking for something the others didn't - information to complete a conflict check. Out of the 40 or so attorneys I had previously contacted, they automatically declined stating a conflict once I gave them the name of my employer.

I gave the attorney the information he requested and I waited uneasy and unsure if the attorney would be able to represent me. While I waited, I continued to organize my evidence and gave thought to a few things. Here's three key things you need to consider when choosing an attorney.

- Employment Law crash course - Employment law attorneys fall into two categories, you have plaintiffs attorneys who represent the employees and defense attorneys who defend the employer. As the employee, you should seek an employment law attorney who has a great reputation for great case results. Beware of websites that feature attorney profiles with ratings. Most of the time, attorneys pay/sponsor priority listings (marketing tool) to boost their profile above other attorneys. Some attorneys will hate this whole section but who cares? I surely don't. The other thing to avoid is the term Super Lawyer, it's another marketing tool attorneys pay for, I know because I've mailed the payments or paid online for those features on behalf of K&B. Also remember YOU are the client which mean YOU are in control and no decision can be be made without your consent.

- What resolution do you want? My mentor Robert Greene gave me a word of advice when I spoke to him about my experience and he encouraged me to "sue the bastards". His advice was simple - start with the end in mind. I had to decide what I really wanted out of this situation. In some cases I researched, the employees wanted their jobs back with the benefits and pay they had. Others wanted a severance and reference letters for other jobs. The final results of your case need to be determined first mainly because it's required when you petition the court to tell them what remedy you want them to grant. There are no wrong answers, I do understand that everyone may not have time to research case results. Set realistic expectations (don't expect apologies written, public or otherwise) and stick to it.

- Questions you should ask an attorney.

    A. What is your success rate, how many cases went to trial and how many were settled?

    B. Do you work on contingency?

    C. What are your percentage rates for representation?

    D. How often should I expect updates about my case?

E. Will I receive copies of all correspondence between you and the defendant's counsel?

F. What requirements do you have for me as your client?

G. In the event, I decide to terminate your firm what is the process?

- Free consultations can be costly - Not all attorneys offer free consultations, be sure to contact them to find out. Employment law is different from personal injury in the way that free consultations are usually limited. In some instances, you will see attorneys advertising free consultations. The amount of time can vary from 10 minutes up to an hour. Get an understanding up front about the consultations policies before proceeding. Make a list of 3 questions you have about your possible case, you may find some attorneys will take up a lot of time talking about other things not relevant to you. The time ticks away and you're left with unaddressed concerns. Treat it as a job interview because that's what it is, you are paying them to represent you and be your advocate. Once you've completed the consultation make a pros and cons list, speak to a few others and hire the one you feel the most confident in.

Takeaways

- **When you consult with an attorney, they have no claim of privilege. That means any information exchanged is NOT covered by attorney client privilege until you have sign an agreement retaining them.** The reason I emphasized that point is because a lot of people misunderstand privilege. Be careful what you share and how much you share because in the wrong hands, the information can be misused or misunderstood. **Do NOT share any proof, documents or recordings until you have signed an agreement.** Sharing can be damaging to your case, I've seen this scenario before and I don't want that to be you.

- When reaching out to attorneys via email, their website etc - keep your first contact brief and to the point of what happened I.e - unpaid overtime (wage theft), harassment, discrimination. **Do not name the company in the initial contact.** Wait for the response from the attorney before sharing additional information.

- Not all attorneys you contact will be interested in your case. Be prepared for declines, it's part of the process. It can be extremely discouraging and frustrating. Trust the fact that your case is worth hearing and your fight is worth it. Take a break when needed, proceed as normal.

I worked with my attorney to ensure things were properly prepped due to my attorney's belief we could settle and prevent litigation. My attorney had numerous conversations with the lead opposing counsel. Unsatisfied with the results of those conversations, my attorney suggested filing suit. I agreed with the decision after speaking at length with him and his associates and having all my questions answered. We filed suit against K&B in October 2014, they were served and I was prepared for the next steps which would be their response and then a hearing. Instead, my attorneys and I were met with threats and sanctions if we didn't dismiss the lawsuit due to a professional courtesy not being extended to them notifying them before filing suit. Livid would be the understatement of the century. Apparently, there is a professional courtesy rule between attorneys where they are required to notify each other of possible litigation.

As I write this, that right there should have been a red flag about my representation. Instead I was livid and upset because of all of it, especially knowing there was close to a $500 loss of non refundable filing fees. I still believe even now it was nothing more than a stall tactic. My team reassured me it was a technicality, I wasn't convinced. That moment changed my perspective on my team and I acted accordingly. I told my attorney the only way I would agree to a dismissal is if it was without prejudice. Without prejudice are two of the most important words in litigation because it gives you the opportunity to file another suit for the same thing in the future. When a lawsuit is dismissed without prejudice, it signifies that none of the rights or privileges of the individual involved are considered to be lost or waived. Once the dismissal was entered, I began to look for other attorneys to represent me. This left me feeling a variety of ways about my attorney, the justice system, opposing counsel and K&B. My attorney moved forward with trying to secure a settlement and was keeping me in the loop of their communications or so I thought.

Plot twist - Let me be windex clear about the next few sentences you will read. I was contacted by someone I trust who told me of a few times my attorney had "off the record" conversations with opposing counsel. To protect that person, I will never reveal which team they worked for. When the person reached out, they gave me details of what the conversations entailed, when they were held and where. I continued providing information as my attorney requested while the possible settlement talks continued.

I made the decision to fire my attorney after speaking with one of his associates who kept pressing me to tell her how many recordings I had. She told me there had been a couple off the record conversations and my attorney just needed to know. The associate continued to tell me since their offices are across the street from each other - they talk about cases from time to time. I let her have it, and told her to standby for an email. I hung up, wrote an email with the subject of Termination of Services. In the email I demanded a copy of my case file, attorney notes, copies of all correspondence and all of my evidence I provided.

Failure to disclose conflicts can be severely damaging to your case, who knows how much information of my case was shared. Only they know, I realized I couldn't trust my attorney anymore so I fired him. He profusely apologized because he thought it was his associates that made me firing him. It was only part of the reason because I had no proof other than the word of my very well placed source. So I said nothing and just observed until the conversation with the associate who I firmly believe was t supposed to tell me. They never knew I was tipped off and watched the way they moved while looking for a new attorney. They know now because they may be reading this just like you are. They were fired in December and I got everything i requested so I could move forward with the case.

In January I found a different attorney who was convinced he could get this settled. He was extremely transparent and I received copies of things as they happened. My new attorney was a solo practitioner who taught EEOC employees and wrote books on retaliation and more. He was and is a fantastic attorney.

Opposing counsel wrote a five page response to my claims and again included a threat of sanctions against my new attorney if he continued to pursue my case and file suit. My new attorney at that point was not willing to move forward in representing me after being threatened. I told him I understood and thanked him.

Completely fed up with the threats from opposing counsel, I understood one thing - Rule 11 wouldn't apply to me. I'm not an attorney, a judge's sanction wouldn't affect my standing with the bar which means they needed to find another tactic. In May 2015, I filed suit again this time more informed and aware and ready for the games opposing counsel would try to play. I paid my filing fees, had them served and prepared for a fight.

Disruptive

A noticeable difference this time around was the case was given deadlines for documents and a hearing date. It's hard to put into words the roller coaster of emotions I felt. Was happy to make progress but weary of the long battle ahead because say it with me - justice takes time.

CHAPTER 06

WHAT TO EXPECT IF AND WHEN LITIGATION BEGINS

*A*ll the work you've done has led you to hire an attorney to represent you in your case against your employer. You attorney has suggested filing a civil action to let a judge resolve the issue. The litigation process can be overwhelming even for the most experienced person. You have to take not only your argument into mind but also the counter arguments the defense can and will have. Your attorney will brief you on what general counter arguments your employer will have. From there, you will both work to strategize and fine tune your argument.

Moment of clarity - Having done litigation work in the past for clients and attorneys, I thought I knew what to expect. I didn't realize how wrong I was, I was prepared for ugliness but nothing at all like what I experienced. My first attorney did prepare me in our lengthy discussions during better terms. One thing sticks out in my mind is this quote "In this case you are calling them racist, sexual predators who posses questionable ethics and cheat taxes. We're in for a fight, you will have to go above your burden of proof to the Court because those are serious allegations which they will vigorously defend their reputations as citizens, attorneys, business

Disruptive

owners and "pillars of their community." The way he broke that down to me was unlike any other lesson I learned.

While there are still hard feelings on both of our parts (you'll see why) I'm forever thankful for that conversation if nothing else. It constantly gave me perspective as I navigated the ugliness of this experience.

Having been to numerous courtrooms, there was something a lot different about walking into a Federal courthouse as a self represented black woman. I became flush with emotion and nervousness, I felt like I was taking all the women of color in with me. As I was on the elevator headed to my hearing, I thought about my grandmothers, great grandmothers and so on who I'm sure we're proud.

I began to panic as thoughts ran through my mind. I second guessed myself, I thought of how much of a fool I would look to everyone. It was a self sabotage moment where I actually thought about not going in. I hit the button for the floor right below where I was headed. I didn't have my phone to call anyone for reassurance - it was just me, my thoughts and my briefcase. I got off the elevator, headed into a bathroom stall and took a few deep breaths. I started to cry because I didn't want to let myself down much less anyone else. As I pulled myself together knowing I was late I said a prayer and paused.

I gave myself 4 deep breaths and told myself to get out of the stall and I thought of my grandmother. Reminding myself of namesake Sarah Mae, my mothers mom who took on the Veterans Administration in the 60s. I'm sad to say I didn't learn this story until after she passed. My Uncle Alvin was a Vietnam Veteran who unfortunately committed suicide while back here in Atlanta on leave. I've never shared this family story because it's so hurtful to my mother, without sharing details, I'll share my grandmother's resilience instead. I have a lot of the same traits similar to my namesake, her get up and go spirit with travel, exploring, her fierce independence, her work ethic and fighting spirit. It annoys my mom now how she will call me and not be sure where I am. Neither my mom nor myself knew where my grandma was when she wasn't home, as we cleaned out her apartment we started to find various Greyhound bus receipts. There were a lot around the Southeast and more than a few to Washington DC and Veterans Administration documents. As I was reading, I learned she was upset the Vietnam Veterans Memorial did not have my uncle's name was not included. She took multiple trips over lots of years and after a long process, she was successful. Her trophy was in her documents, she took a pencil and paper with her to trace a copy of his name in the wall.

With that in mind, I got back on the elevator, took a few deep breaths and opened the door to walk in to my hearing. I walked in alone but not really alone if that makes sense. I was reprimanded by the judge about my tardiness, I apologized and blamed it on parking. I sat at the table like you see on tv with the microphone and pitcher of water. I poured a glass of water, pulled up my chair, turned on the microphone and embraced my inner Annalise Keating.

The hearing was scheduled because the judge wanted to give us his rules (each judge has their own), his expectations from us, deadlines for filings and to address the questions we had. This hearing was a lot of firsts for me including my first time meeting the opposing attorney. Once the judge gave his requirements, he opened the floor for us to speak. As I attempted to ask the questions, I was constantly interrupted by opposing counsel who kept belittling me stating "she's not an attorney so she doesn't understand." The judge reprimanded him, before I continued I asked the judge if he thought I had trouble comprehending and he smiled and said "no, you may continue uninterrupted." The next question I asked was

Disruptive

if I could submit the certified audio recording from the GDOL where K&B testified they fired me. The objections were loud and rapid because K&B's attorney obviously didn't know about their testimony. He was overruled and the judge said he would love to hear it because K&B swore under penalty of perjury I abandoned my job. I walked out of there feeling victorious and ready for battle.

Crash course of the litigation process cause Google can be overwhelming - If you've made it this far with your attorney, you're paying them to worry about this. Here's a quick breakdown of the process.

- **Discovery** - My judge gave us a standard 3 month discovery period some judges give more of you request it. Because I had my evidence already in place, I focused on interrogatories, RPD's, and RFA's. All of which leads up to the deposition and helping to narrow questions you pose during depositions. Here's a quick breakdown of each. Interrogatories are series of questions you require answers to in writing. Request for Production of Documents (RPD's) are the documents you want them to provide, in that document I also requested recordings, videos, and emails. In turn, they asked for the same but also requested text messages which I objected to due to my expectation of privacy in which The Privacy Act of 1974 supports that argument and thus upheld. Requests for Admissions (RFA's) are written requests to admit or deny various things that took place. After going back and forth with the initial round, there was a second round of interrogatories, RFA's and RPD's we went through before the deadline approached.

- **Work product privilege** - I knew I had all the same rights as attorneys in this matter due to my pro se status (self representation). The problem came when I didn't provide what opposing counsel demanded and cited work product privilege. I politely suggested to them instead of trying to give me an education, they should refresh their own knowledge first. Time passed and this became such an issue to them during my deposition, they called the judge on me lol. More on that in a minute.

- **Discovery conclusion** - We reached the end of the contentious and full out ugly discovery period. Ugly because a lot of false personal attacks on my character and I vigorously defended myself while calling them all types of liars. The next phase was deciding on depositions, we had spoken to the judge and identified the month in which we should be completed. Dates were set and I left the option open and filed a Notice of Deposition to depose Baer.

- **The Deposition** - Leading up to this point, I had to file a warrant application for criminal harassment for threats I received and the ignoring of my repeated requests for one the attorneys to stop contacting me. The Rambo style tactics and lawyering they had been conducting and trying to get away with was unacceptable. (Want to make an attorney mad, use that term and watch how indignant they become) I watched they way they tried to do that in Eve's legal proceedings (having her followed by private investigators, continued harassment etc.) Again, we were each other's witnesses in that part of both of our litigation proceedings. It became extremely ugly and I had to file a lawsuit with the county magistrate. Needless to say they were fully aware by that point I would not tolerate any further foolishness or stunts. My deposition was scheduled first, there were a few things I knew not to do or take with me:

  - **A. Do not take your cell phone into the deposition.** Some attorneys will wait for you to pull out your cell phone, wait for you to look up information saved and then request access to your phone to find something to use against you. Opposing counsel thought I brought my phone in but were disappointed when I left it in the car. Even if they had made a stink, called the judge and demanded an instant decision, I would've cited 1974's Privacy Act as my defense and reiterated that discovery had already closed.

- **B. Do not take notes during the deposition.** This is another major key, you may have an attorney who requests a copy of your notes, it's highly intrusive (right to privacy) and you may have to object and argue it letting a judge decide. It's worth arguing, when and if that happens, the deposition is usually paused while the arguments are given and the judge rules. The deposition will resume.

- **It is ok to refresh yourself on things before the deposition, you may be asked the last time you looked at case related material.** After using questionable tactics to get me unfocused at the start of the deposition, (like offering condolences on the loss of my mom - still alive btw) to get me off my game, I was asked the last time I looked at case related materials. The fake and misplaced offer didn't knock me off my game it made me decide gloves were off and proceeded to answer them. Always being under the assumption I was "getting help" from someone (no brain of my own perhaps) I confirmed no one helped me prep and the truth doesn't change and doesn't need remembering.

There were a few times I was threatened with calling the judge, my response was let's do it. I had refused to reveal my employer. I still maintained it shouldn't be their business because I didn't work for K&B any longer. I lost that round and provided the information. It left opposing counsel shook because they realized I upgraded to a global firm where they knew the types of litigation I worked on which varied from transactional, civil, criminal, financial, employment, civil rights and liberties cases. It gave me a very vast knowledge on quite a few areas of law which allowed me to research case filings, preparing discovery, compose discovery documents.

My new employer's resources were at my fingertips and allowed me to be over prepared for my case against K&B. Opposing counsel also knew I signed an NDA and couldn't do more than provide the name of the firm and my start date. My new firm had no idea of my litigation against K&B and still doesn't. It wasn't anybody's business but my own and I kept it that way. Opposing counsel was quite incensed, they realized I didn't have any help but I had the ability to learn, research and apply what I learned. That made things all the more contentious.

After they requested multiple breaks to go pow wow with Baer (who was there the entire time) they came back all upset. Questioning continued, we reached another disagreement opposing counsel's voice was raised as he slammed his hands on the table. I laughed at him and replied in my most condescending voice "you're becoming quite combative aren't you?" That part of the transcript always makes me laugh because he intended that to be me acting a pure fool and it was him. He threatened to call the judge and as I continued to laugh and drink my tea I told him let's do it again!

The judge took a deep breath and exhaled with so much disdain, resentment, annoyance and anger. I smiled because I felt the same and knew opposing counsel was on thin ice. Opposing counsel stated I was refusing to answer questions and citing privilege. He tried to question my understanding and then told the judge to compel me to answer. After the judge took another deep breath, he asked did I really consider the information work product privilege. I said yes and gave him this scenario: if attorneys were required to share vital defense and evidentiary information with each other

Disruptive

there would be no need for a Justice system. If I shared vital details, I thought it would be only fair for opposing to share theirs and then go from there.

I asked the judge if that made any sense and would there even be a need for trials, judges, and juries. He simply responded to me "you've made a compelling argument I'm inclined to agree with you." He ruled in my favor to keep my work product privilege assertion. I thanked him and apologized for the disturbance and told him I hope we wouldn't need to call him back. *As a pro se litigant, you have the right to claim privilege on any case related material you feel qualifies. If opposing disagrees, let a judge decide. Do not share anything you feel opposing can take to try to use against you.*

You know what happened next? Opposing called another break, when they returned I asked if they would pay for my parking since we were there so long. I answered questions for another 20 questions, Baer paid for my parking and offer lunch I declined and we were done. They had the option to recall me for more deposing, they never did. After reflecting on that day, I declined to move forward on deposing Baer because out of all of this, their written responses plus the GDOL testimony was more than enough to prove my case.

Takeaways

- A. Expect your employer to make you look like the worst employee in history. It's litigation, there will be character questions raised on both sides. The goal is to convince the judge or jury to rule in your favor. Arguments always have the potential to get heated and escalate quickly, your attorney will advise you to remain calm and let them handle it. During hearings, most reasonable judges will have to remind both sides at least once to keep the case about facts. You can request the attorney to ask for a break if you need time to collect yourself.

B. Expect to tell your side of the story multiple times and vigorously defend your character during this process. Personally, it's highly irritating for me to constantly repeat myself. As your case prep begins, you will be asked by multiple people to tell the story from your perspective. It's not that your attorney doesn't believe you, sometimes you remember a detail you hadn't before etc. The purpose is to get you ready for the questions from the opposing counsel team.

C. Expect to feel like this is the longest process in history. Our justice system and its processes can be extremely lengthy. Depending on the complexity of the case, the Court may give you deadlines that are months away. Your attorney will work with you to prepare you for depositions, prepare sworn statements, interview possible witnesses and gather. Deadlines matter, filing the day after your deadline can get your case thrown out. Be sure to understand how the court calculates days. In some courts, days include the weekend days. Extensions can be granted, sometimes over the phone stay on top of deadlines.

We proceeded to wrap up discovery, I noticed opposing counsel inserted some of Eve's deposition from her proceeding in my case. I filed a motion and requested a subpoena for the full deposition because context matters. By the time the judge was ready to review my request, discovery was over and I was denied. It was a loss, on the brighter side, at least it's on record I tried. The most important takeaway about litigation is knowing you can win some, lose some but never forget why you did it.

CHAPTER 07

KEYS TO KEEP IN MIND WHILE LITIGATING

*A*fter our discovery period closed, months passed and we entered a new year. There was still no updates or decisions made on the case. It was fine because life was happening. I lost my father, dealt with job and family stuff while waiting on a trial date from the court. It was the toughest period of my life and while I dealt with a new normal, I waited for the judge's next order. Opposing counsel filed a motion for summary judgment stating my case was frivolous and I didn't meet my burden of proof. Out of 6 recordings (which included K&B's testimony of firing me) and hundreds of documents, it's laughable to say I didn't. For every affidavit they filed, I gave proof why those documents were not only untrue but subject to penalties of perjury. One of my coworkers who signed an affidavit wasn't even employed at the time I was fired but gave an account of what happened. In my opposition to summary judgment, I pointed out each thing wrong with their argument of my case being frivolous. I added my proof (documents, recordings) a third time along with a detailed table of contents as list of exhibits properly labeled.

Earlier I wrote to plan for the end, here's the reason why - in case of a need to appeal. I knew my next filings would have to be all inclusive and as concise as possible in case I would need to appeal.

Having researched all possible ways this could go, even with all of my evidence and proof - the judge could rule against me. Everyone that knew about this case thought it would be impossible for me to lose because that GDOL hearing testimony by K&B was hard to fight. I felt differently in my gut for a few reasons - I was pro se, I was taking on well established attorneys and the judge I was assigned didn't have a history of being plaintiff friendly. All judges have reputations for the way they rule and how they examine cases. I hoped in my own case, I would be victorious. I filed my opposition and waited knowing I would possibly need to appeal.

I had researched my options for the appeals process including the filing fees, differences between the courts and most importantly how long I would have to file the appeal. If you have an attorney, expect to have these conversations about plans after litigation. Some attorneys may be reluctant to talk about losing but it's a reality you should discuss.

Months went by, clerks changed and I needed to take a leave of absence from this case to handle my father's estate. I filed the documents and submitted proof of the county court's records in my request. Usually when you file a leave of absence, it can take a few weeks for the court to review and grant or deny. While I waited to hear back, instead the judge made a ruling for summary judgement and dismissed my case. Talk about a shock.

I was so taken aback by his reasoning for dismissing my case he said it was because I didn't prove I experienced an "adverse employment action" after complaining about unpaid overtime, racial discrimination, reporting the sexual assault and speaking to the IRS about the employment taxes which led to retaliation.

Here's what an adverse employment action is: An adverse job action is an employer's action that affects an employee's job negatively. Losses of pay, termination, or demotion are all examples of adverse job actions. ... An adverse job action "must be materially adverse, meaning more than a mere inconvenience or an alteration of job responsibilities."

Most people who could not believe the judge's ruling all asked the same question. So being fired doesn't equal an "adverse employment action"? Apparently not to the judge over my case. For the sake of argument, take away the GDOL recording (which was never ruled inadmissible) there were documents I filed from the GDOL confirming my firing. Additionally, I filed the recording of the meeting where you could hear us being fired and told to leave the office.

Knowing I repeatedly filed all of that evidence, gave me peace of mind to heavily consider an appeal. I also knew because the judge was never asked to rule my evidence inadmissible, opposing couldn't ask for it during the appeal. That's a prime example of what happens when you don't stay on top of your game. This became a major argument during the appeal.

Here's my take on what possibly happened, I don't think the evidence was reviewed. One of the times I filed the recordings and documents, the judge reprimanded me for not "organizing and labeling properly". I believe the judge did not listen to or read the documents even after filing the properly labeled evidence. Otherwise, what would explain his ruling that I wasn't fired? Most of the time, judges are not so hard on pro se plaintiffs because judges understand pro se plaintiffs are not familiar with the rules and procedures. My judge was tougher on me and honestly more liberal with opposing counsel. They were never held accountable for knowingly submitting untrue statements from "witnesses" etc. I had pointed it out as rebuttals and provided proof and that was "overlooked".

Takeaways

- **The court needs time to review all of the documents each side has filed.** During the course of discovery, each side could file hundreds of documents. If reviewed properly, it can be a while before you get an update. Patience is key. Your attorney will ensure everything is properly filed within the rules of the court. You can request a copy of the documents filed on your behalf. I encourage you to get a copy of everything you can because you need to have it.

- **The case clerk is your new best friend.** If you're pro se, make sure to keep in touch with your case clerk. He/she is the gatekeeper and can follow up on your behalf. Keep in mind there is a slate of cases assigned to each clerk and judge. Always keep your case number handy to make it easier for everyone. Because I was pro se, it was my responsibility to keep in touch with my case clerk. Clerks are rotated so there may be a new one assigned. I had two different ones while my case was in District Court and quite a few in Appeals. Case clerks cannot give legal advice but can suggest steps you can take or court documents that can help you. I honestly would not know a lot of the things I learned early in my case if not for my clerk. Ask questions, take their suggestions.

- **A lot can happen while you wait on a judge's decision.** Attorneys can file motions for summary judgement, dismissal etc to prevent your case from moving forward. Motion for Summary Judgement asks the judge to evaluate the case and make a decision without a trial or a jury. This is why your evidence is important. Motions to Dismiss asks the Court to dismiss the case because it's frivolous or you didn't meet your burden of proof and keeping it open is a waste of time. ***You as the plaintiff, have the burden of proving your case meaning you have to prove what you're*** *saying happened actually did.* You prove that with witness statements, deposition testimony, emails, photos, recordings etc. Y*our former employer has no burden to meet, it's all on you and your legal team.* Throughout your legal process, keep that in mind and again expect a counter argument to poke holes in your account.

The Next Steps- Hearing to determine moving forward. The court will notify you of a hearing date to give instructions on dates for trial, jury selection, and expectations. The judge may also offer dispute resolution as an alternative which is also called mediation. In some cases, a judge may offer mediation to let all parties try to agree on a result without litigating further through trial. Trials can be time consuming, jury selection can be lengthy and starting the trial can take months to years. If both parties are open to mediation, the judge will make an order to complete by a certain date. It's not a requirement and sometimes, parties don't agree. In my case, mediation was not something opposing counsel was open to and I wasn't either.

Preparing for mediation - Mediation is usually conducted by a neutral third party in a conference room type of setting. Both sides give opening statements and start discussions on how to resolve the issues. You can accept or deny an offer if you don't agree. Your attorney will do most of the talking and advise you. This process can take hours. If both parties can't agree, the case goes back to the judge. If you are pro se, you will have to decide what it will take for you to walk away. I would advise researching case results for your type of case to get an idea of what cases like yours settle for. I was able to gain a better valuation of what a case like mine had reportedly settled for so I could be better prepared with my expectations.

BONUS

My Appellate Experience

The disappointment in the judge's ruling didn't last long because I had to focus all my time and energy into my appeal. I struggled with self doubt and negative self talk about if an appeal was something I could really do. I had conversations with close friends trying to decide if it was something I was ready to take on. There was a lot of turmoil in my personal life at the time. I was still grieving my father when I had to start a legal battle with his widow. A few of my personal relationships were irreparably damaged, had to cut off a lot of people during this period. It was an emotional time and I was uncertain.

The bottom line was, less than 30 days from the judge's ruling to decide to fight it let this go. At that point in the case, I had invested over 3 years into this fight. I decided to consult a few attorneys to see if I could hire representation to relieve myself of another round of litigation.

Appeals are a different game with different rules and more rigid procedures.

Crash course on Appeals and Appellate Court proceedings -

A. Know the rules before start - There are a few things you need to know about the Appeals process. First, there's a new ***non refundable*** filing fee due to the Circuit Court. My filing fee was $500.00, I had to file my Notice of Appeal within 30 days including my reason for the appeal.

B. Your reason for appeal has to meet one of three standards. Those three standards are:

- You believe the lower court made a legal error, you're asking for the ruling to be reversed. Legal errors are somewhat common, although most judicial officials try hard not to make mistakes. We are human, sometimes it happens. You could also argue like I did, the evidence wasn't properly reviewed and didn't consider all the facts of the case. My argument was the judge erred in deciding I didn't suffer "an adverse employment action" and dismissing the case.

- Question of law - The most interesting and sometimes frustrating thing about the law is: we can read the same ruling and interpret it differently. This issue happens frequently which is why arguments are made. Your argument can be an incorrect interpretation of the law was applied and explain your reasoning in your argument.

- Abuse of discretion - A judgment will be termed an abuse of discretion if the judge has failed to exercise sound, reasonable, and legal decision- making skills.

With each of these standards or grounds for appeal you will need to have a strong, valid argument. Your argument will need case citations proving why your argument is the one the appeals court should rule in favor of.

My argument is after all I submitted including paycheck stubs showing I wasn't paid overtime, I wasn't awarded anything.

Manage your expectations - Your Notice of Appeal is just the first step in appealing your case. Keep in mind Circuit Courts adjudicate cases from multiple states. I filed in the 11th Circuit which serves Georgia, Florida and Alabama. The appeals process is extremely time consuming and the rules are extremely strict. Once your notice has been filed, you will receive documents from the court with your case number, filing instructions and deadline information and rules of the court. Here's a timeline of how a case proceeds through appeals court.

- **Required documents** - You will need to complete a transcript request and submit it to the District Court. I filed my Notice of Appeal with my District clerk who gave me the transcript form to complete right there. The transcript is important to your appeal because the Appeals Court only reviews what was filed on the record. **The Appeals Court does not review new evidence.** If it's not in the record, it will not be reviewed.

- **Preparing your brief-** There are a lot of rules regarding the preparation and filing of your brief. The most important rules to adhere to is font (Times New Roman) and size (14). Line spacing should be double. There are page limits, my brief couldn't be over 20 pages check your rules from your court. Lastly, I had to provide seven copies of the brief and appendix to the court for filing. The cover had to be gray and the binding had to be correct, I chose spiral binding. The reason you have to provide so many copies is because you have 3 judges who will review it. Additional copies are backups and remain with the clerk. You also have to provide a copy to opposing counsel. Reply briefs have the same rules, your cover has a different color requirement.

- **Appendix is everything** - Your appendix should any relevant documents that support your argument and grounds for appeal. **Include only what supports your argument, label it properly and file it on time. Your case will be dismissed if your appendix is not filed on time.** You can submit an addendum to your appendix if you left something out, don't panic. You will have a chance to file a reply brief and an additional appendix before the case moves forward. Once all the of the briefs have been filed, the case will move forward for review. While it's being reviewed, you may receive updates from the Court on what and if they need anything additional. Appeal Courts will make a decision in writing for your case, your case may be referred back to the lower court to proceed to trial. Conversely, the Court may made a ruling to end proceedings; hope for the best and prepare for the worst.

Here's what's happened since filing the Notice of Appeal with the 11th Circuit Court. I took my time writing my appellant brief because it was vital to get it right. I poured over the evidence I filed myself again because I had to refresh and make my argument concise. I drilled down to three points of my argument to develop my grounds for appeal. My argument was the evidence wasn't properly reviewed, the standard was the District Court erred in dismissal of my case.

"The District Court erred when it decided I wasn't entitled to be paid overtime wages. I provided paycheck stubs that showed 82 hours, I was paid straight time for all hours. I wasn't paid overtime for 2 hours on that paycheck. In total I wasn't paid for 167 hours of overtime. If the District Court reviewed the paycheck stubs, how could they rule I wasn't entitled to payment?"

I already mentioned how the court decided I didn't experience an adverse employment action by being fired. In my Appellant brief, I cited the evidence I filed 5 times from the GDOL including recordings and their letter of the investigation results proving I was fired. Additionally, I provided the recording of the mandatory firm meeting where everyone could hear us being fired. I believed the court erred in that decision.

With regard to the racial discrimination count, I pointed out that even after providing Eve's affidavit detailing discrimination the court never considered the evidence. With racial discrimination complaints there's a term used called prima facie which means on its first appearance. It's defined as: based on the first impression; accepted as correct until proved otherwise. Another definition: on its face," referring to a lawsuit or criminal prosecution in which the evidence before trial is sufficient to prove the case unless there is substantial contradictory evidence presented at trial. All opposing counsel stated was it wasn't true. My argument was they didn't provide contradictory evidence. For that reason, I argued the court erred in the decision I didn't prove my claim.

My argument for my retaliation claim was the same as it was regarding was for everything else. I was retaliated against for complaining of racial discrimination, reporting the sexual assault and calling the IRS which led to me being fired. If the GDOL agreed why didn't the District Court?

Life happened, I had to call the clerk to ask for an extension on filing my appendix. The extension was granted over the phone and I was able to file it on time. Opposing counsel filed their brief regurgitating the same arguments they gave to District Court and claimed I didn't meet my burden. I was given the opportunity to files reply brief. Dealing with life and a few challenges, I almost didn't file a reply brief. I felt my initial brief was great and could stand on its own. Speaking with a confidant about where things stood, I decided to file a reply.

Disruptive

My strategy for filing my reply was to attack each argument opposing counsel made and provide proof to counter. Each affidavit opposing submitted, I countered with evidence to prove perjury. Perjury was the word I had avoided the whole case, it was all or nothing at this point. I argued the statements of Laura should be impeached because she has resigned the day before we were all fired. How could she provide a sworn statement giving details about our firing if she wasn't there? With the affidavits Kalka & Baer provided they lied about the circumstances of my firing. On top of that, the sworn affidavits they filed were signed after their DOL testimony. How could you swear to two versions of the truth? I argued their affidavits were nullified and their testimony to the GDOL should be the only testimony considered. I argued all of their affidavits should be impeached and their lack of credibility be heavily considered. My reply brief was my last chance to get everything on the record and my last chance to convince my three judges I was right.

I suffered a medical emergency which caused a first for me, I missed the deadline to file my appendix for my reply brief. The clerk dismissed my case, I was devastated and that was it. There was a mix of emotions, I tried to collect my thoughts and started researching a way to reinstate my case. I received the dismissal, I noticed something in the letter that prompted me to call the clerk. I asked if I could file a motion to reinstate along with the appendix to try to move the case forward. My clerk gave me a strict deadline to file. I filed my motion and appendix and waited for a decision.

Weeks went by and I battled serious anxiety which didn't help my health issues. I knew if the judges didn't reinstate the appeal, I failed at giving a strong argument for them to consider. Three weeks later, I received an order from the court with 2 judge's signatures **granting** my motion to reinstate. I had convinced 2 judges my appeal had merit and deserved to be considered. Three judges review the appeal, knowing that I felt like I won. I felt vindicated and an overwhelming wave of emotions. I called the clerk to get insight into the next steps. As we were wrapping up the call, I began to cry happy tears and I thanked her.

A few weeks later, I received a letter from the court I nervously opened it. It was a letter advising opposing counsel to file an entry of appearance. I was baffled so I called the clerk and asked "weren't they supposed to file this first before any briefs?!?!" She confirmed it was supposed to be filed at the start of the appeal. She confirmed it was filed, I thanked her for two things. First I thanked her for all she had done and sharing her knowledge with me. Secondly, I thanked her because it proved someone in the court was finally paying attention to this case to notice a missing filing. I asked if anything else was needed and she told me everything was going to the judges the next day. It's been in their hands since and as of the publishing of this book there's been no ruling yet.

Epilogue

*I*t's been a long road to get to the place of now realizing everything that's happened so far has made me who I am. I firmly believe the mantra "it's either a blessing or a lesson." It took me a long time to realize that about my experiences and adopt that mindset. We all have our crosses to bear and all have our own walk. At a few points I thought I cried all the tears I ever and will have. I lost a lot throughout this process, in exchange I gained a lot of knowledge. The key for me was through it all I never lost my faith - in myself, God and the journey as a whole. I'm thankful to my tribe for uplifting me when it was hard to hold my head high.

The experience of being subjected to toxic work culture, speaking out and challenging that system is not easy. Standing up for myself and others was an easy call that I would make again. Accepting the consequences of that is part of the process. We all know for every action, there's a reaction. I've had to repeatedly defend my character each time it was called into question by opposing counsel. The fight has been extremely messy and sometimes unpredictable.

One thing I've always said and will continue to say to those who defend K&B to me is if I'm lying and making it up why haven't they sued me? They've had 4.5 years to sue me and never have. If someone was lying publicly about you, you wouldn't sue to clear your name? I honestly expect some form of threat about this book. I'm prepared as always for the "backlash", threats of lawsuits and maybe injunctions. I look forward to defending myself as always because I didn't sign an NDA. I chose to be silent about my experience because I wanted to. I feel differently now, I want to help others who may not have resources I did.

As I bring this book to a close, I want to thank all the people who tried their hardest to discourage me. Whether it was pursuing this case, filing criminal warrants in a separate action etc. thank you. I was told by so many people I had no case. I was frequently reminded of the story of David and Goliath. "You're in over your head, you don't know what you're doing. You can't take on 2 attorneys and their legal team. They are not going to let a college dropout beat them. You're not equipped to battle them etc." Every time I was given that comparison and even when I get it now, I smile and say "All David needed was faith and a slingshot, don't believe me just watch."

www.ingramcontent.com/pod-product-compliance
Lightning Source LLC
Chambersburg PA
CBHW021506210526
45463CB00002B/915